WESTLEY, THE Big TRUCK

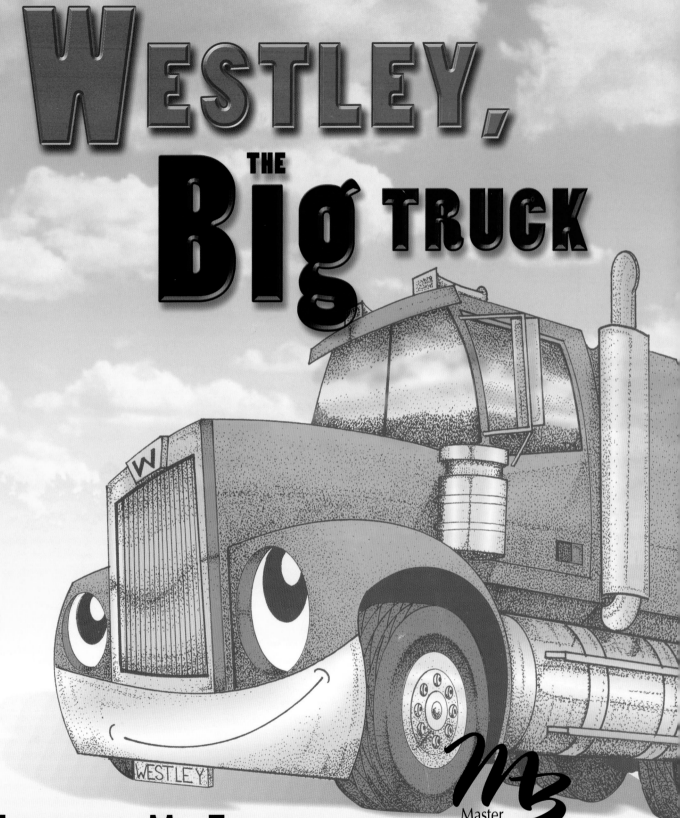

James McEwen

Master Books

A Division of New Leaf Publishing Group

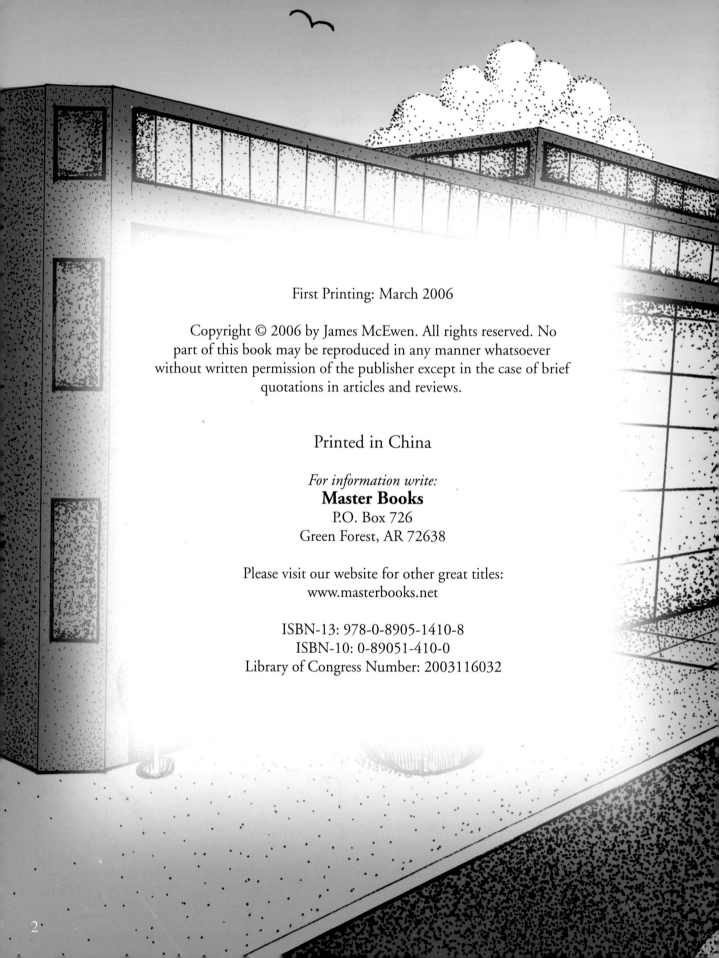

First Printing: March 2006

Printed in China

For information write:
Master Books
P.O. Box 726
Green Forest, AR 72638

Please visit our website for other great titles:
www.masterbooks.net

ISBN-13: 978-0-8905-1410-8
ISBN-10: 0-89051-410-0
Library of Congress Number: 2003116032

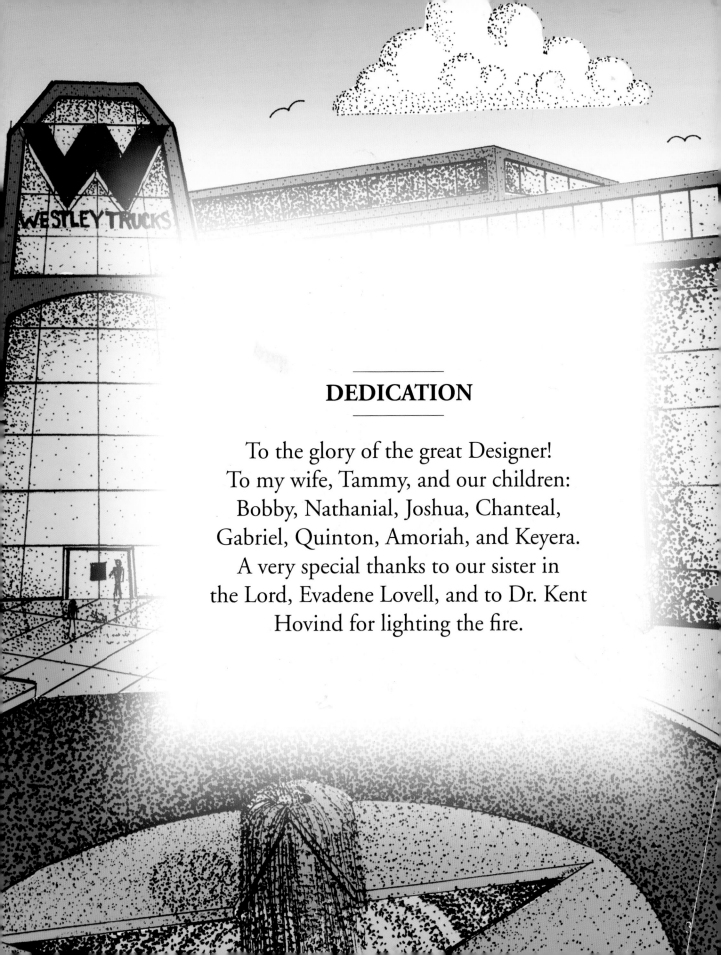

DEDICATION

To the glory of the great Designer!
To my wife, Tammy, and our children:
Bobby, Nathanial, Joshua, Chanteal,
Gabriel, Quinton, Amoriah, and Keyera.
A very special thanks to our sister in
the Lord, Evadene Lovell, and to Dr. Kent
Hovind for lighting the fire.

The storm clouds were black and rolling in fast as Westley, the big truck, was coming into Big City. As usual, he was happy. He was right on time with his weekly load.

As he headed toward his destination, he passed the many businesses on Main Street: the Check With Us First National Bank, the Curl Up and Dye beauty salon, the Refreshing Paws pet shop, the Eat Em & Weep Cafe, and his favorite place, the Tanks-a-Lot gas station. Westley had been there so many times that he knew this part of the city very well.

As Westley approached the traffic light, it turned from green to yellow, and Westley's air brakes hissed as he slowed and came to a stop. As Westley waited, he could see that the storm clouds were very close, almost right overhead, and he could hear the rumble of thunder.

The cross traffic finally cleared the intersection and the light turned green. Traffic began moving on the other side of the intersection and in the lane next to Westley, but Westley didn't move — he couldn't. Something was wrong.

Since Westley was not able to move, the vehicles began to come around him very slowly in the next lane, one by one. Even through the heavy rain, Westley could see that they were not happy. Some of the snooty foreign cars sneered at him as they passed, and the other big trucks looked away sadly as they came by him.

A gang of loud motorcycles went around
him, shouting insults as they passed like:
"Ya big lump of junk! Get it out of the road!"
and "You ain't nothin' but a heap of scrap!"

A tow truck came and took Westley to the garage. Westley was silent as he was put in a bay, and men began to work on him. An older and wiser truck named Diesel was in the next bay, and when he saw how sad Westley was, he said, "Hey, what's the matter, kid?"

I guess I'm just a pile of junk," Westley replied. "I'm no good. I came from a scrap heap and I'm going to the junkyard."

"Whatever gave you that idea?" asked Diesel.
"Well, it's true, isn't it?" whined Westley.
"Well, let me tell you a story," replied Diesel,
"and we'll see what you think after that, okay?"
Westley just looked at the floor.

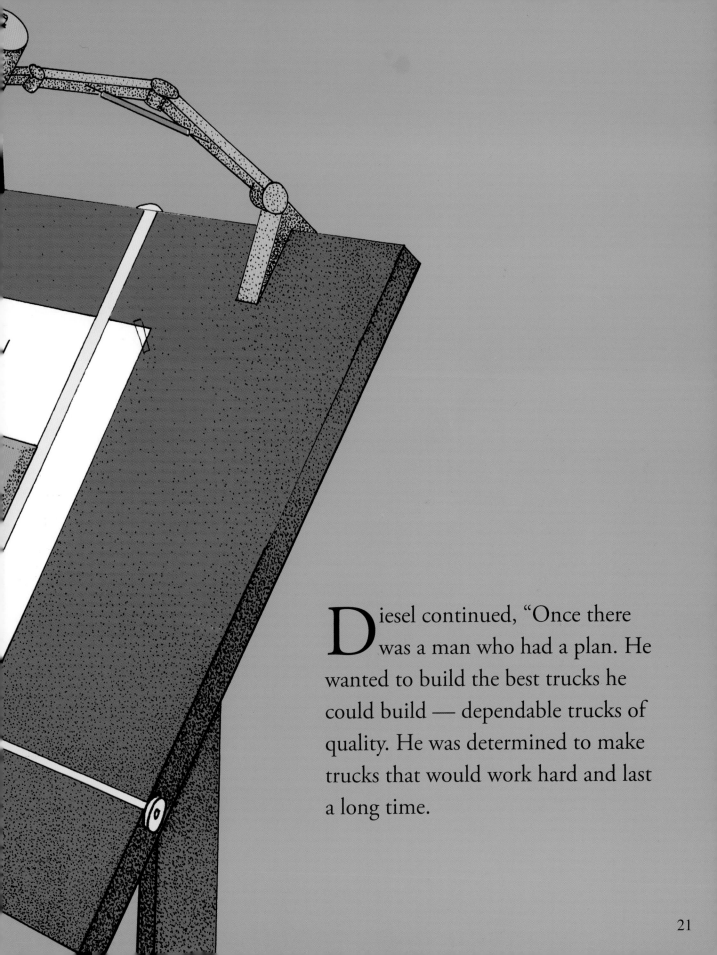

Diesel continued, "Once there was a man who had a plan. He wanted to build the best trucks he could build — dependable trucks of quality. He was determined to make trucks that would work hard and last a long time.

He didn't start out by going to a junkyard to get some old, cheap scrap metal for his trucks. No, he found the best materials and he built a wonderful factory and hired people to build the trucks. He discovered that the most practical way to put trucks together was by using an assembly line.

The first step is for smart engineers to invent a code system (special instructions just for you), which other people can use to help them understand the plans of the engineers.

Then, using that
code system,
the engineers draw up blueprints, which are special drawings
that tell how to build you. Once the
design is perfected and sent to the factory,
all the parts are brought together. And because
the factory workers know the engineers' code,
they can read the blueprints and know how
to put together a truck, step by step.

First, a sturdy frame is made that will be the base for every other part of the truck.

Next, the axles that will hold the wheels are attached to the frame.

Then, the frame and axles move into a "spray booth" where they will be painted.

One of the most important parts is added next — the engine, which provides the power. Without it, the truck could go nowhere!

The cab, where people sit and drive the truck, is assembled.

Then the cab is dropped into place.

Ten tires are mounted onto the truck. The trailers pulled by these trucks have eight wheels, making eighteen altogether, which is why they are sometimes called eighteen-wheelers.

The headlights and grill are installed and the big hood is lowered so it acts as a cover to protect the engine.

The new truck leaves the factory — the Westley Truck Factory — as a perfect, shiny work of art, beautifully designed and assembled with great care," Diesel said.

Diesel looked at Westley, "And that's where you come from, my boy. You were carefully designed and then put together using the information from the engineers' blueprints. Complex machines like you and me can't form on our own! And living things are even more complicated than us trucks — they also had to have been carefully designed and created."

Just then, the mechanics closed Westley's hood. "We're finished. This Westley is as good as new!"

As Westley left the garage, he said, "Thanks, Diesel!" and his bright chrome seemed to shine brighter than ever in the sunlight that had come after the rain.

There were no clouds in the sky as Westley went on his way.

<u>Resources</u>

Just as Westley had a designer and creator, so do you!
The Bible talks about how God designed and created the
whole world about 6,000-10,000 years ago.

For you created my inmost being; you knit me together in my mother's womb. I praise you because I am fearfully and wonderfully made; your works are wonderful, I know that full well. My frame was not hidden from you when I was made in the secret place. When I was woven together in the depths of the earth, your eyes saw my unformed body. All the days ordained for me were written in your book before one of them came to be. Psalm 139:13-16 (NIV).

God knew who you were before you were even born and He specially designed and created you for a purpose! To learn more about creation, talk to your parents and read the following Scriptures with them.

Genesis 1
Genesis 2:18-25
Genesis 3:1-10
Exodus 20:8-11
Job 38
John 1

Resources for study and reflection:

www.answersingenesis.org
www.icr.org
www.drdino.com
www.visionforumministries.org

Interactive 3-in-1 Books that Teach Kids about Character

Fun four-book series
by award-winning producer
Tony Salerno

Children follow the adventures of little Bill and his friends as they learn through experience the values and benefits of good character. These books are large, containing full-color cartoon illustrations that tell the complete story, and include an audio CD with the complete animated narration of the story with exciting sing-along songs.

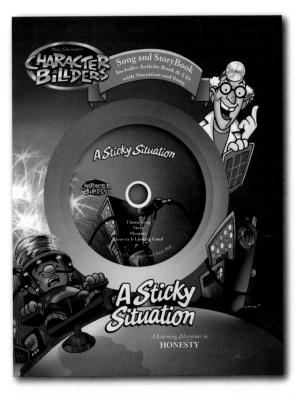

A STICKY SITUATION
A Learning Adventure in HONESTY
Tony Salerno
0-89221-606-9

Also included in each book is a 30-page (reproducible) activity section and song lyrics. Parents, grandparents, and educators will find these books to be terrific resources for building balanced character qualities. Each book is hours of fun for children 6–12.

WHERE'S BEEPER?
A Learning Adventure in HELPFULNESS
Tony Salerno
0-89221-603-4

WISE QUACKS
A Learning Adventure in SELF-CONTROL
Tony Salerno
0-89221-604-2

"Available at Christian Book Stores Nationwide"

Children 6–12
60 pages each + CD w/each
Hardcover • Color interior
$14.99 each

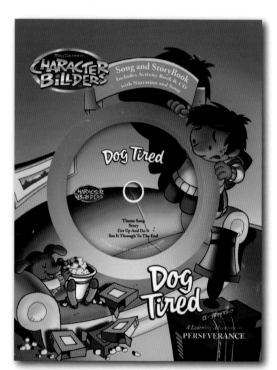

DOG TIRED
A Learning Adventure in PERSEVERENCE
Tony Salerno
0-89221-605-0